Alderman John Bowen J.P.
'Honest John'

Founder of John Bowen & Sons Ltd.
Builders of Victorian Birmingham.

Anthony Collins

John Bowen as High Sheriff of Worcestershire 1916 - 1917

Alderman John Bowen J.P.
'Honest John'

Founder of John Bowen & Sons Ltd.
Builders of Victorian Birmingham.

Anthony Collins

ISBN 978-0-9930538-0-1
© Anthony Collins, 2014.

Published by
Anthony Collins Publishing
134 Edmund Street
Birmingham B3 2ES

Designed and printed by
Adlard Print & Reprographics
Ruddington, Nottingham
www.adlardprint.com

The illustration of John Bowen on the cover page is from 'The Dart', 24th July 1891, by kind permission of Birmingham Archives and Heritage.

Introduction

John Bowen was my great grandfather. I grew up with family stories of him having been born in Rochford, a village near Tenbury Wells, and reputedly walking into Birmingham as a carpenter with a sack of tools on his back. He started a business and went on to build the Victoria Law Courts in Corporation Street.

Very little else was known. Now retired, I have spent the last five years or so following up my fascination for my ancestor by researching archives and contacting all my first and second cousins on my mother's side of the family. In the course of this and in giving lectures on his life and work I have come across three former employees of John Bowen & Sons Ltd and have written some 90,000 words on his life and of the firm. This opus is not yet ready for publication as I am aware that there is much more to find out and research.

The purpose of this little book is to whet the appetite of those interested in the entrepreneurs of Victorian Birmingham, hopefully to find and flush out memories from former employees and to learn from historians who may be able to add to the list of buildings that I know John Bowen & Sons Ltd must have built.

Acknowledgements and Dedication

There have been very many people who have helped and encouraged me with my intended book, too many to mention here, but whom I wish to mention when the larger book is published.

For the moment I would like to dedicate this book to Val Hart and Chris Sutton of The Balsall Heath Local History Society, both of whom have enthused about John Bowen and his contribution to Balsall Heath, who have assisted me with my research, and who have been kind enough to show their excitement at all that has been discovered so far. Balsall Heath has a proud and noble history and has many fine buildings, particularly on the Moseley Road and which are now sadly run down. It is only by walking the Moseley Road that you can really appreciate the wonder of these buildings and the need for inward investment. Val and Chris work hard at promoting Balsall Heath by ensuring that the present diverse community is brought together, by appreciating the history of the area, and by demonstrating hope in what an individual with hard work can achieve. I am privileged to be an honorary member of their Local History Society and hope that this little book will aid them further in their endeavours and encourage others to do the same for the communities in which they live and work.

In the meantime there is much delight in Balsall Heath that Birmingham Civic Society is to put up a blue plaque to honour the part that John Bowen made in the development of Birmingham, and I thank Christine Cushing as Chair of the Society for joining me to promote this and The Wesleyan Assurance Society for sponsoring the blue plaque.

Anthony Collins, September 2014.

John Bowen (Birmingham Archives and Heritage)

Catherine Julia Bowen née Townsend, John Bowen's second wife.

The glass used by Queen Victoria when laying the foundation stone of the Victoria Law Courts on the 23 March 1887 and acquired that day by John Bowen for five shillings.

The Armorial Bearings of John Bowen prepared by the College of Arms and granted on the 22 February 1916. John Bowen's heritage and shooting interests are reflected by the woodcock as the crest, the Welsh lion with the freemasonry square and compass, and the pears of Worcestershire. Using the word 'built' in the motto maybe an intentional pun but doubtless expresses something of the man himself.

The Tenbury Wells National School in Cross Street, which John Bowen attended until the age of around twelve. It is likely that he would have had to walk to school each day from the village of Rochford; a distance of approximately two and a half miles.

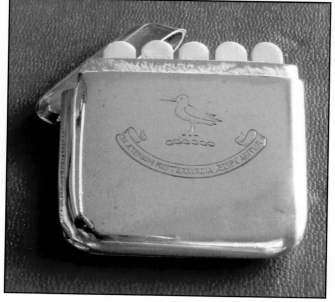

John Bowen's shooting pegs engraved with the woodcock from the crest of his coat of arms and his motto, 'Mercy shall be built up for ever'.

John Bowen with Sir Alan Cobham at an air show at Bingley Hall.

THIS GUN, SUPPOSED TO HAVE BEEN USED BY THE ARMY OF OLIVER CROMWELL, WAS DUG UP SEPT? 1884 WHILE EXCAVATING IN THE OLD PRIORY BIRMINGHAM NOW CALLED PRIORY PLACE.

A Civil War cannon supposed to have been used by the army of Oliver Cromwell which was dug up when John Bowen & Sons were working on the Priory Site in the Old Square in 1884. John Bowen had the cannon restored and kept it at 'Rochford'. Sadly the cannon was subsequently melted down during the Second World War in support of the war effort. I wonder if Oliver Cromwell would have approved.

The lady is Marjorie Moore with her daughter. The Moore family bought 'Rochford' from the Bowen estate.

John Bowen leaving his home 'Rochford' in Strensham Hill, Moseley, wearing his High Sheriff court dress. The car is a Wolseley Siddeley which he purchased new in 1909. This enormous car was painted dark lake and weighed one ton and twelve hundredweight.

The Rt. Hon. Gisela Stuart M.P. and Anthony Collins with John Bowen's gift of Dame Laura Knight's painting of Sennen Cove entitled 'Autumn Sunlight' on loan to No 10 Downing Street in April 2012. The painting was bought and donated by John Bowen to The Birmingham Art Gallery in 1923.

A BIRMINGHAM GOLDEN WEDDING.

Alderman John Bowen and Mrs. Bowen, of Rochford, Strensham - road, Moseley, who yesterday celebrated their golden wedding, having been married at Edgbaston Parish Church on 7 May, 1874.

John and Catherine Bowen celebrating their Golden Wedding at Edgbaston Old Church on 7 May 1924.

John and Catherine Bowen's grave at Brandwood End Cemetery. The author is intending to have the grave restored shortly.

Alderman John Bowen J.P.

Founder of John Bowen & Sons Ltd.

John Bowen was born on the 16 December 1844 in Rochford, a village two and a half miles from Tenbury Wells in Worcestershire. His father, Thomas, was a blacksmith and ran the smithy fronting the road in Upper Rochford.

The Bowen family had lived in Rochford for at least four generations, and in the wider area for over two hundred and fifty years, tracing their roots back to 1695. John was the sixth of nine children and with an elder brother likely to go into the business, it must have been pretty clear to him that there would not be room for him in the family blacksmith shop and that he would need to leave home to find other work.

Having attended Tenbury National School in Cross Street, John worked initially as a cow boy at a local farm until in 1868, at the age of twenty three, he walked into Birmingham. He may well have served an apprenticeship as a carpenter either in Tenbury or Worcester before he came to Birmingham.

Initially he lived in 'digs' in Latimer Street South near Holloway Head, an area lived in by a number of Welsh families. On the 24 October 1871 he married Sarah Ann Spencer at the local Methodist Church of St Asaph's and the newly married couple moved to live in Tindal Street in Balsall Heath. The following year on the 10 August 1872 a son John George Bowen was born, but tragically Sarah died only a few days later on the 29 August. Their baby son, John, survived lived only a year and then he too died on the 11 July 1873, an event sadly not uncommon in those days.

On the 7 May 1874 John Bowen married again, this time to Catherine Julia Townsend. Theirs was thankfully a long and happy marriage, and Kate, as he called her, went on to bear John nine more children: Albert, Kate, Arthur, William, Ethel, Florence, Maud, Thomas and Leslie. Three of the boys, Albert, Arthur and Tom, went into the business; William became a surgeon at Addenbrookes in Cambridge; Maud died in childbirth; and Leslie became a solicitor, but was killed in the First World War. Florence was the only one of the four girls to marry.

John Bowen's initial move to Balsall Heath may have been due to the active building trade and brick works in the area, because his first wife's family lived in Moseley, or perhaps both. In any event, after the birth of his first son Albert, he leased property in Edwardes Street, Balsall Heath, now known as Edward Road, and built a home for the family together with a builder's yard next door. His building business was under way by 1875 and it accelerated at a pace.

It is not clear how exactly John Bowen started off in the building trade. He clearly had skills and was by that stage a Master Carpenter, but it is most likely that he took leases of land which became available for building in the area and built villa properties which he later sold on. At that time it was usual to take what is known as a building lease for ninety nine years at a low or 'peppercorn' rent with an obligation to build a property of a certain value. The builder would then sell on at a profit and the lessor would retain the freehold as an investment receiving a small annual ground rent, having received a capital sum when the lease was granted to the builder.

One of the first buildings known to have been built by John Bowen is The Red Carriage Bridge, which spans the two pools in Cannon Hill Park. This contract may have been due to John Bowen being referred to Sir John Holder who lived in a large mansion known as 'Pitmaston' and whose grounds adjoined Cannon Hill Park. Sir John also donated land to add to the Park following Louisa Ryland's gift to the City in 1873. John Bowen was later to carry out extensions in 1878 to Sir John's brewery in Nova Scotia Street and carry out other work for him.

Whilst John Bowen had initially started by building villas, he soon concentrated on more prestigious buildings and began winning public contracts to build some of the Board Schools, public baths, factories and churches.

Birmingham's building trade was booming and in the years between 1870 and 1902 fifty two Board Schools were built and John Bowen is known to have built at least four and probably a great number more. These include Kings Heath School in 1877, Tindal Street in 1879, an extension to Mary Street in 1883 and Lower Broadway School in Aston in 1899. The majority of these schools were designed by the architects Martin and Chamberlain and many of these wonderful terracotta buildings are still in use as schools today.

In 1880 John Bowen bought for £2,250 the premises in George Street which John Smith junior, and his father before him, had been running as swimming baths. This purchase served him well over the years, providing him with offices and a joinery yard. Around the same time in 1883, he moved his family from Edwardes Street to a new and larger family home which he built at the corner of Edgbaston Road and Strensham Hill, calling the new house 'Rochford' after his village home. Never seeming to stop in taking opportunities, he also bought other land in Strensham Hill and Strensham Road, building at least ten more houses which he retained as an investment.

Other investments in 1882 were two parcels of land on the Moseley Road which were later to form the site of the Moseley Road Baths. He sold some of this land in 1894 to the Corporation for the building of the Baths for £2,539/19/0. He must have been disappointed not to have won the tender to build the Baths himself as he had built the Monument Road Baths in 1881. He later went on to build Nechells Baths in 1910 and most likely built others too.

Some of John Bowen's contracts were for factory buildings and included the Mozart Piano works in Ombersley Road, Balsall Heath, in 1889 and the Perfecta Seamless Tube Factory in Plume Street, Aston, in 1918.

But it was not only schools, baths and factories that were being built, but churches too. John Bowen attended the Wesleyan Church on the Moseley Road, which may have been another reason for initially moving to Balsall Heath. Although he did not build that church, he was a trustee of it and played a significant part in extending the circuit of Moseley churches.

The Wesleyan churches built by the firm include the Asbury Memorial Church in Holyhead Road in Handsworth in 1884, the Kings Heath Wesleyan Church in Cambridge Road in 1896, the Hart Memorial Church in Gravelly Hill in 1890, and the Wesleyan Church in Hazelwell Road, Kings Heath, in 1910. He did not exclude himself from building for other denominations and built for the Congregationalists a church in Ladypool Road in 1907, and, for the Anglicans, the Grade I St Agnes Church on the Stratford Road in 1899. For the Catholics, he built St Patrick's Church on Spring Hill in 1885 and, after John Bowen's death, the firm built an extension at St Edmunds Church in Raddlebarn Road, Selly Park, in 1939.

Nearer to his home in Moseley he had by then built the Moseley and Balsall Heath Institute in 1882 and at the time of his death he was its longest serving member. In and around Birmingham he built the Edgbaston Assembly Rooms at Five Ways in 1883, the extension to the Art School in Cornwall Street in 1891, the Birmingham Meat Market in 1895, and Cornwall Buildings in Newhall Street in 1897.

There are not many parts of Birmingham in which John Bowen has not left his footprint, but in terms of the number of buildings in one part of town, this must unquestionably be in Corporation Street. It was under Joseph Chamberlain's leadership when he was Mayor that he enabled Corporation Street to be carved out of the slums and drove a new street through from New Street to Lancaster Circus, clearing the slums under the authority of the 1875 Artisans Dwelling Act. Work began in 1878 and Chamberlain's new Parisian Boulevard to be known as Corporation Street was opened up as far as Bull Street by 1881 and later extended to Lancaster Circus. The Improvement Scheme was paid for partly by the sale of leases on the street but due to the economic slump of the early 1880's the buildings beyond The Old Square comprised for the most part public buildings such as the Victoria Law Courts and the Methodist Central Hall both of which John Bowen built.

Corporation Street must have seemed like one enormous building site in those years. John Bowen could not have been in business at a more opportune time and the firm built at least twelve sizeable buildings between the years 1886 and 1901 in Corporation Street and Old Square. These included department stores and two Central Halls for the Wesleyans. The feather in the cap of John Bowen will always be as the builder of the grade 1 Victoria Law Courts, the foundation stone of which was laid by Queen Victoria on the 23 March 1887. When the law courts were finished they were reputed to be the finest in the country, and John Bowen would be proud that they are still in use today. All these buildings demonstrate John Bowen's skill both as a builder and a businessman who was able to win contracts of this size.

At the turn of the century John Bowen's tender of £207,256 won him a huge contract to build Hollymoor Asylum at Rubery which took up the years between 1900 and 1905. Not being content with a contract of this size, it is amazing to discover that during this time John Bowen voluntarily served as chairman of the building committee of another large asylum at Barnsley Hall which was being built at Bromsgrove by another local builder B. Whitehouse of Edgbaston.

With Hollymoor being completed in 1905, the firm then went on to win the contract to build yet another asylum at Netherne, near Croydon, between 1905 and 1910. The value of this contract was even larger and in the region of £300,000. The management of this contract from Birmingham in the days before electronic communications must have made huge demands on logistics and many of the Bowen family were drawn into helping out.

Around that time John Bowen & Sons Ltd was building Hockley Post Office in 1911, the Birmingham Repertory Theatre in 1912 and an extension to the Queen's Hotel at New Street Station in 1914. Other contracts were for the Midland Bank and with the General Post Office for the Telephone Exchange.

It is likely that John Bowen started to retire around the age of 60 in 1904, but it is hard to imagine that he took his hand off the wheel. He had formed the company of John Bowen & Sons Ltd, possibly around the early 1900's, and the firm was now being run by his eldest son Albert Bowen aided by his brothers Arthur and Tom. The formation of the limited company was no doubt concurrent with the next generation taking over the firm, but it seems extraordinary to us today that a builder would take on contracts such as the Victoria Law Courts without the protection of limited liability.

He had a built up a company with an enviable reputation and was known as 'Honest John', which is perhaps the best accolade anyone can have in business.

During his life John Bowen was involved in a great many charitable causes and public duties which included -

- Taking an active interest in the work of The Building Federation. He was president of the Birmingham Master Builders Association in 1884, and held the office for three successive years. In 1894 he occupied the highest position in the trade as president of the National Federation of Building Trade Employers of Great Britain and Ireland and was re-elected to this position the following year. When the Midland Federation was constituted in 1898 he was elected first president and held the office for two years.

- In April 1880 he was elected a member of the Balsall Heath Local Board. He served on all the committees in turn and officiated as chairman of the Heath Committee. In 1883 he was returned at the head of the poll and was elected as chairman. In the 1886 election he was returned unopposed by Balsall Heath ratepayers after six years valuable service, but two years later he resigned his seat on the Local Board because of differences over litigation in which the board were involved.

- He was a member of the Tame and Rea United Drainage Board for two years.

- On the formation of Worcestershire County Council he was elected as Councillor to the Balsall Heath South Division in January 1889. Having re-joined Balsall Heath Local Board John Bowen remained a member until the absorption of Balsall Heath under the Greater Birmingham scheme on the 1 October 1891. At that time he was elected an Alderman for the County of Worcestershire and devoted himself to County Council work in Worcestershire.

- In 1892 his name was added to the Commission of the Peace in Worcestershire on the recommendation of the Earl of Coventry sitting until the annexation at Kings Heath court.

- He was chairman of the committee of Barnsley Hall Worcestershire County Asylum for 21 years until 1923 and gave advice as to the selection of the site and the construction of the buildings. The builder had suggested stone but John Bowen recommended terracotta reducing the materials cost from £9,000 to £8,000. The estimated cost of the building works was £152,000 but the actual costs were £10,000 less and the architect said that such a thing had never been heard of before.

- He was granted his own Coat of Arms in 1916 by the College of Arms and a stained glass window with the Bowen Arms is included, with those of other High Sheriffs of Worcester, in the Shire Hall in Worcester.

- He occupied the position of High Sheriff of Worcestershire in 1916-1917.

- He was a Freemason Master of the Fletcher Lodge 1031 and in 1889 subsequently presided over the Fletcher Royal Arch Chapter. He had the unusual distinction of having occupied both the warden's chairs in the Provincial Grand Lodge of Warwickshire.

- He was actively interested in the Moseley and Balsall Heath Institute serving one year as president. He joined in 1882 and was elected a Vice President in 1893 and was instrumental in obtaining a grant from Worcestershire County Council for £400 in 1892. He was president from 1916 -1918 and a trustee from 1896. He was a generous supporter of the Institute's work in which he took an active interest and at the time of his death was the oldest of its 911 members. He was a also a member of the Council of Kings Heath and Moseley Institute by virtue of his membership of Worcestershire County Council, formerly made a grant for educational purposes.

- He was a generous man. For many years he was interested in Wesleyan Methodism and played a prominent part in church extension to which he contributed generously. His financial contributions towards extending the Moseley Circuit of the Wesleyan Church included paying for the tower of the Wesleyan Church in Cambridge Road, Kings Heath, with his wife, Kate, donating the rose window and altar screen. He later attended St Anne's Church, Park Hill, Moseley, to which in 1917 he presented the Church with a handsome lychgate in memory of his year of office as High Sheriff of Worcestershire and in 1922 he gave a beautiful baptistery as a thank offering for a long and happy and successful life. Also in 1922 he bequeathed to Birmingham Art Gallery the painting 'Autumn Sunlight' by Dame Laura Knight. Dame Laura was one England's foremost female artists of the twentieth century and the painting was loaned by Birmingham to 10 Downing Street in 2009. On his death he bequeathed £1,250 to the Birmingham General Hospital to endow a bed in memory of his youngest son Leslie Harold Bowen who was killed in France in 1915.

- The Dart periodical on the 24 July 1891 stated that 'there is no more noteworthy example of success among our citizens – a success achieved by sterling integrity, unflagging energy and shrewd business common sense - than that afforded in the career of the subject of this brief sketch.'

- Another newspaper article says of him that he was one of the most prominent figures in the Midland building trade and noted for his long association with the public life of Balsall Heath. He was a self-made man, possessing a genial temperament and was a considerate employer. It was reported that it was no longer a secret that, as a consequence of his popularity and of the good name he enjoyed in Birmingham, he was freely spoken of as a successor to the then late Liberal M.P. Mr Powell Williams as Member of Parliament for South Birmingham. It was reported that he felt himself, however, unable to give this time and attention which parliamentary work required and was content to pursue his public work in the local sphere in which he had rendered such extremely useful service.

Although John Bowen stepped back from active control of the business around the age of sixty four, he nevertheless continued to take a strong interest in the building trade and modern building methods of the day, taking his wife and daughters to America in 1909, sailing on the S.S. Campania, where he studied the construction of skyscrapers.

The Second World War years then followed and the firm was kept going with government contracts under the direction of his son Albert. After the First World War the firm was never quite the same, and further deterioration took place after the Second World War. The firm moved out to Knowle and built houses in the area but still continued with some notable building projects building the Colonnades, which are now in the Peace Gardens in Holloway Head, and laid out the grounds for the Hall of Memory in what is now Centenary Square in 1923. The Hall of Memory was built by another builder John Barnsley & Sons, a firm with which John Bowen had traditionally competed and it seems appropriate this the work on this site was shared between them, as each had lost a son in the First World War. Between the two wars John Bowen & Sons Ltd built The Beacon Insurance Building in Hall Green in 1937 and during the Second World War carried on with government contracts for work at airfields and army camps at Honeybourne, Long Marston, Bicester and Nesscliff as well as building prefabs in Selly Oak.

After retirement the climax of John Bowen's life was being installed as High Sheriff of Worcestershire in 1916, Moseley still being within that county at that time. The Bowen Coat of Arms which he had been granted was also something of which he was immensely proud and he incorporated these arms on almost everything from stained glass windows to the side panel of his Wolseley Siddeley motor car.

He and his wife Kate lived to celebrate their golden wedding anniversary in 1924 with a service at Edgbaston Old Church, before having a party with his family at 'Rochford', toasting the occasion with a glass of lemonade. His children clubbed together with a gift of an Elkington Rose bowl similar to the ladies' trophy at Wimbledon, inscribing their names on the stand.

All things good things and lives come to an end and after an illness with prostate cancer John Bowen died on the 26 April 1926 in his eighty second year. The coach hearse with its black horses collected his body from 'Rochford', and after a service at St Anne's Church in Park Hill, took his coffin to Brandwood End Cemetery where he was buried in a grave with a marble Celtic cross, to be joined just two years later by his wife on the 1 March 1928.

Although he had instructed Alban Buller, a fellow Wesleyan, as his solicitor in the early days, his will was drawn up by the Birmingham firm of A. H. Coley & Tilley. At the time of his death he was chairman of City Arcades (Birmingham) Ltd, Cornwall Buildings Ltd, Edwin Fletcher and Co., Ltd, managing director of the Birmingham and Midland Val de Travers Paving Company Ltd, and of course formerly Chairman of John Bowen and Sons Limited. His estate included shares in Birmingham city centre property companies, ownership of a number of houses in Moseley and of farms in Leigh Sinton, Worcestershire, comprising approximately one thousand acres. His gross estate was valued at £134,027 with personality of £70,077, a not inconsiderable sum in 1926.

The firm of John Bowen & Sons Ltd carried on under the leadership of his son Albert Bowen and was managed by him through the Second World War, whilst Albert's sons were away in the services. With the war over, Albert became increasingly interested in hunting with the hounds and enjoying his hobby driving coaches. The firm was taken over by Albert's youngest son Patrick Bowen who had returned from the war; but business was difficult and the entrepreneurship of its founder was missing. Ultimately, and to the distress of the family, John Bowen & Sons Ltd finally went into administration in 1963 whilst working on a subcontract at Five Ways, Erdington.

Whilst John Bowen & Sons Ltd is sadly typical of many family business which only survive three generations, John Bowen has left us with a tangible legacy of many quality and historic buildings which are still in use today and which we can literally look up to and admire as they represent all that is good about Victorian Birmingham.

John Bowen's life demonstrates what it is possible to achieve by hard work, good fortune and honesty; 'Honest John' in name and deed. I am sure that his Christian faith and upbringing as a Wesleyan had a great deal to do with what he was able to achieve and I am proud to be one of his great grandchildren.

A sample of buildings that John Bowen built
The dates shown are the start of the contract if known, but, if not, when the building was opened.

1875. The Red Carriage Bridge, Cannon Hill Park.

This is the first known structure to have been built by John Bowen and is in Cannon Hill Park. The land to form the park was donated by Louisa Ryland in 1873. It is probable that John Bowen won the contract as a result of his relationship with Sir John Holder who lived at 'Pitmaston' in Moseley, and who also donated adjoining land to add to the park.

1877. Kings Heath Board School, Kings Heath High Street.
(Mary Harding post card)

Designed by William Hale. Demolished in 1981. This was one of a number of Board Schools built by the firm and stood on the corner of Institute Road and Kings Heath High Street. The winter of 1978 did irreparable damage to the school buildings which were demolished in 1981 when the school moved to Valentine Road.

1878. Holder's Brewery, Nova Scotia Street, Birmingham.
(Photo - Birmingham Archives and Heritage)

John Bowen built an extension to Holder's Brewery which later became part of Mitchells and Butlers.

1879. Tindal Street Board School, Balsall Heath.

Designed by George Ingall. The contract cost was for £6,356 10s.

John Bowen lived in Tindal Street with his family before moving to 16 Edwardes Street (now Edward Road) . The School is still proudly in use today and known as The Ark Academy.

1882. The entrance to the George Street joinery yard.
(Photo - The Balsall Heath Local Historical Society)

John Bowen acquired the land in 1880 for £2,150 on the 6th October 1880 from the family of John Smith who for many years had had a swimming bath on the site.

The gable to the gateway building still bears the initials of John Bowen, recording the building in 1882. The terracotta is probably from Ruabon. George Street was developed in stages, with John Bowen submitting plans for 'Shopping' in 1887 and 1895 for three storey offices and joinery shops on this extensive site which would have been needed, not least, for the building of the Victoria Law Courts.

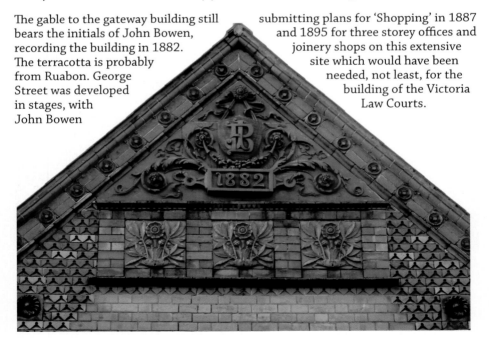

Corporation Street, Birmingham.

1880. The Marris and Norton Building, 19 -21 Corporation Street.
(Mary Harding post card)

Designed by Martin and Chamberlain. It is believed to be the existing building with the pink striped awning and coloured grey.

1881. Monument Road Baths, Ladywood.

Designed by Martin and Chamberlain.

This is the first record of the many public buildings built by the firm and enhanced John Bowen's reputation as a builder.

During the winter months the Birmingham baths were boarded over and used for social functions such as dancing. This building was demolished in 1945 and replaced by new baths on the site which were also subsequently demolished.

1882. The Moseley and Balsall Heath Institute, Moseley Road.

Designed by William Hale. The Institute was originally formed in 1879. John Bowen was a member from 1882 and President in 1916-1918 and at the date of his death in 1926 the oldest member. His children held their twenty first birthday parties at the Institute.

1883. The Mary Street Board School extension, Balsall Heath.

(Photo Balsall Heath Local Historical Society)

This was the first school in Balsall Heath to be built by the school board and the cost of the extension was £4,297. The school was badly damaged in the Second World War, renamed Belgrave school and was demolished in 1970. Mary Street school was replaced by Heath Mount Primary school also in Mary Street but on the opposite side of the road.

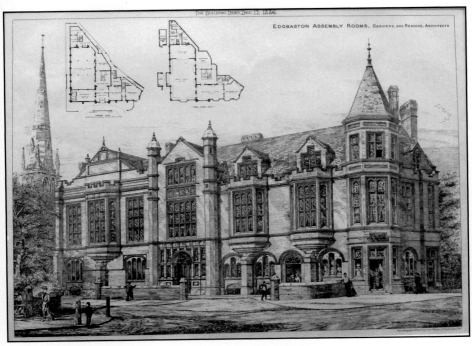

1883. The Edgbaston Assembly Rooms at Five Ways.

Designed by Osborne and Reading who also designed John Bowen's house 'Rochford' the same year. Now demolished, it was originally on the present site of Tricorn House at Five Ways. The Building was used by both the Freemasons and also Sir Barry Jackson for rehearsals for his Pilgrim Players before the Repertory Theatre was built.

1883. 'Rochford', Strensham Hill, Moseley.

Designed by Osborne and Reading. John Bowen's family home from 1883 until his death in 1926. This photograph was taken after a billiard room was added on the right hand side. John Bowen also built at least ten houses in Strensham Hill and Strensham Road, retaining them as an investment.

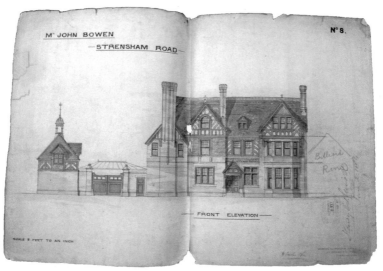

One of a set of Osborne and Reading's architectural plans for 'Rochford' discovered with the deeds. (Courtesy - The Family Housing Association).

'Rochford' is now demolished and forms the site of social housing.

1884. The Bishop Asbury Memorial Church, Holyhead Road, Handsworth.

Designed by Mr L. J. Ball. The first minister, the Rev K. W. Briggs, wrote a book on Asbury's life and raised funds for the church in America. Bishop Francis Asbury (1745 - 1816) was one of the first two Bishops of the Methodist Episcopal Church in the United States. As a young man in October 1771, Asbury went to America and during his forty five years there, devoted his life to ministry travelling thousands of miles on horseback and by carriage to those living on the frontier.

The church original originally had a steeple which was demolished in 1954 as it was deemed to be unsafe. This was hardly surprising as the church had suffered bomb and fire damage both in the First and Second World Wars.

The church is still in use today and is now run by the New Life Wesleyan Church.

1885. The Roman Catholic Church of St Patrick Spring Hill, Dudley Road.

Designed by Dempster and Heaton.

The church is in the French Gothic Style of the 12th Century. The inside is stunning and deserves a visit.

1886. The Jevons Buildings, Corporation Street, which housed the Liberty Store

(Photo - Liberty and Westminster City archives)

Designed by William Hale.

Built on what is now the site of 'The Square Peg' in Corporation Street and backing on to the Minories, the building was of Tudor style and used red terracotta. It was occupied by the London firm of Liberty's. Doubtless John Bowen was appointed in view of his relationship with Samuel Jevons who was a fellow Wesleyan. Unusually, the building was supported internally by oak posts instead of cast iron columns which were felt preferable in case of fire. The Birmingham Daily Post described the building as one of the most picturesque in the town.

1886. The Wesleyan Schools, Lime Grove Balsall Heath.
(Photo Balsall Heath Local Historical Society)

Designed by William Hale. The buildings comprised an Assembly Hall with sixteen classrooms but are now sadly demolished.

1887. 25 - 27 Corporation Street, Birmingham.

Designed by Dempster and Heaton.

Originally occupied by Pattison - Hughes Catering Co. Ltd. with a shop and a restaurant on the first floor.

1887. Houses in Strensham Hill, Moseley.

Designed by William Hale and others.

John Bowen built a number of houses on the eastern side of Strensham Hill, immediately opposite his family home 'Rochford', as an investment which he retained until his death. He also built others in Strensham Road.

1887. The Victoria Law Courts, Corporation Street.
(Photo Mr. David H. Bradnock M.B.E., J.P.,D.L.)

Designed by Aston Webb & Ingress Bell and listed as Grade 1.

The land was acquired by Birmingham Corporation in 1883 and the foundation stone was laid by Queen Victoria on the 23 March 1887. The Courts were opened by the Prince of Wales on the 21 July 1891.

The final cost amounted to £113,000. When opened The Victoria Law Courts were described as the finest modern building in the country. This magnificent building is still in use today, providing the country's largest magistrates courts complex. The flaming red terracotta was made by J. C. Edwards of Ruabon and, after standing for over hundred years, there is not a shrinkage crack to be seen.

The Great Hall of The Victoria Law Courts. (Above)

The interior is equally majestic and whether or not required by the law demands a visit. It is a mixture of French Renaissance with Gothic content.

The hall measures 80 x 40 feet, is embellished by stained glass windows and has buff terracotta supplied by Gibbs and Canning of Tamworth. Dominating the space are two great arched entrances with a French Renaissance character, massively surmounted by lions and unicorns supporting the Royal Arms.

Three of the stained glass windows of The Victoria Law Courts. (Left)

The middle of these stained glass windows in the Great Hall of the Courts show the foundation stone being laid by Queen Victoria standing with the Lord Lieutenant, Lord Leigh, and Thomas Martineau. The man shown with the mason's trowel is unfortunately not John Bowen, but Mr Davies, the clerk of works.

1887. The first Wesleyan Central Hall, Corporation Street.

Designed by Osborn and Reading. This building was on the north eastern corner of Old Square. Built with a main hall to accommodate one thousand, it was found after ten years to be insufficient for the Wesleyans, who then built the second Wesleyan Central Hall opposite the Victoria Law Courts. The original foundation stone recording John Wesley's preaching at the Cherry Street chapel, is now in the basement of the second Central Hall.

1889. The Mozart Works. Ombersley Road, Highgate.

Originally built for Sames Pianos and now occupied by the Islamic Help charity, this is one of a number of industrial buildings that John Bowen is known to have built. Another was for the Perfecta Seamless Tube Works in Plume Street Aston. The Mozart building caught fire in 1913 and again in 1923 from the sparks of passing trains on the adjoining railway.

1890. 'Glen Lyn', 6 Park Hill Road, Moseley.

Probably designed by William Hale and built at the rear of the garden of 'Rochford' at the corner of Park Hill and Edgbaston Road. Park Hill was cut in 1865 so it would have been sometime before this plot was developed. This house was another house built as an investment and one of a number inherited by the author's grandfather, Arthur Bowen, on the death of John Bowen. The house is now divided into flats.

1890. The Hart Memorial Church, Gravelly Hill. (Mary Harding post card)

Designed by Messrs Ingall and Sons in a Gothic style. Now demolished, the church stood at the junction of Gravelly Hill and Kingsbury Road and the site is now occupied by flats. The church had seating for five hundred and was built for the United Methodist Free Church and named in memory of Alderman M.J. Hart.

1890. Manchester Buildings, The Old Square. (Mary Harding post card)

Manchester Buildings is the red terracotta building with awnings in the far distance. A strange name for a Birmingham building.

1890. Princess Chambers, 2 -12 Corporation Street, Birmingham.

Designed by Dempster and Heaton for the Clarence Property Company. This building fronts the junction of Corporation Street with New Street. Sadly it has lost its adjoining neighbours, the majority of which suffered war damage and were redeveloped as part of the Big Top site.

1891. The extension to the School of Art in Cornwall Street.

Designed by William Martin and John Henry Chamberlain the Cornwall Street extension numbering nine bays was an improvement to the 1884 Art School, the main building having been built by William Sapcote. The cost of the extension was £11,697. Owing to a bricklayers strike lasting thirteen weeks, the contract overran and took two years to build.

1893. The Kyrle Hall, Sheep Street, Aston.

(Photo - Birmingham Archives and Heritage)

Designed by William Bidlake.

The facade was of red Leicestershire sandstone and was of a semi- Elizabethan design. The hall had a capacity for five hundred and cost £3,835.15.0 to build.

The Kyrle Society was founded in 1880, with the object of bringing natural and artistic beauty to the lives of the citizens of Birmingham and no doubt contributed to the Arts and Crafts movement. Sadly this building was demolished.

1893 - Edgbaston Vestry Hall, 176 Islington Row.

Islington Row was originally called New Bridge Street and this building stood on its junction with a small road known as Enfield Place. The Birmingham Daily Post on the 27 January 1893 described the building with its Oriel window as having Red Beggars Wall dressings and stated that John Bowen had taken over this contract from C.W. Barker of Edgbaston who had died. This building was demolished in the widening of Islington Row.

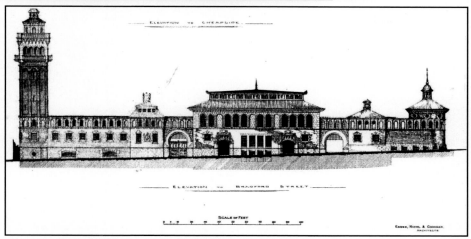

1895. The Birmingham Meat Market, Bradford Street.

Designed by Essex Nicol and Goodman. In the early nineteenth century the clearance of buildings allowed the markets to be developed in this part of town. This extensive building for the meat market with an accompanying slaughter house was opened in 1897.

**1896. A. R. Dean.
153 - 161
Corporation Street,
Birmingham.**

Designed by Crouch and Butler. A. R. Dean was a furniture store and this building originally encompassed their showroom on the ground floor with a vegetarian restaurant on the first floor. The buff terracotta balustrades contain motives of carpentry and wine making. Still standing today, the building now provides offices for solicitors as it is conveniently located close to The Victoria Law Courts.

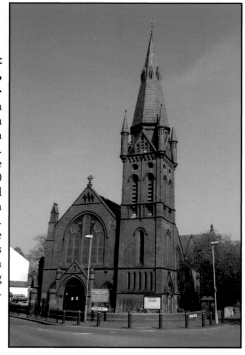

**1896. The Wesleyan Methodist
Church, Cambridge Road,
Kings Heath.**

Designed by William Hale. John Bowen was one of the trustees involved with the expansion of the Moseley Wesleyan Circuit, of which this church forms part. He not only contributed £700 for the building of the tower but donated £100 towards the cost of building Spark Hill Methodist Church and Hazelwell Church both of which are now demolished. His wife Kate Bowen paid for the rose window and the altar panels. It is believed that some of these terracotta bricks may have been surplus following the building of the Victoria Law Courts.

1896. Newbury's. The Old Square, Corporation Street, Birmingham.

Designed by Essex Nicol and Goodman. Newbury's was a Birmingham store fronting the Old Square, bordering on what is now the 'Minories'. Note the tramway leading into the Square.

1897. Cornwall Buildings, 43 - 51 Newhall Street Birmingham.

Designed by Essex Nicol and Goodman, Grade 2. John Bowen was Chairman of Cornwall Buildings Ltd and had the benefit of a mortgage on Cornwall Buildings at the date of his death. He probably built this building as an investment with other entrepreneurs.

1898. The City Arcades. Bounded by Corporation Street, Union Street, New Street and the High Street. (Mary Harding post card)

Designed by Essex Nicol and Goodman. Listed as Grade 2*. John Bowen was Chairman of City Arcades (Birmingham) Ltd and the arcades, which were funded by a consortium of businessmen, were almost certainly built by John Bowen. At his death he owned shares in the Arcades which suffered extensive bombing in the Second World War, although the frontages and a short part of the arcade leading from Union Street remain.

1898. 'Domus', Half Key, Malvern.

'Domus', was John Bowen's country house. Used by him as a shooting lodge, it resembles a Moseley house of the time, but is surprisingly small. Stabling at the rear enabled the horses to be kept close to the thousand acres of farm land with several farms that he owned on adjoining land which he bought in 1898. Terracotta owls form part of an unusual feature of the roof and the porch contains oak panels with Latin inscriptions. His initials 'J. B.' are installed on the wooden timbers on the frontage and the windows still contain his stained glass.

1899. Broadway Lower School, Whitehead Road, Aston.

Designed by Crouch and Butler. Listed as Grade 2. This was one of the Board Schools in Aston and has some magnificent terracotta work including a sundial. The Bromsgrove Guild supplied the mural of St Augustine and the copper foundation plaque which hung in the entrance naming John Bowen as the builder was assuredly also made by the Guild.

1899. St Agatha's Church. Stratford Road, Sparkbrook, Birmingham.

Designed by William Bidlake. Listed as Grade 1. The church suffered bomb damage in the second world war but the church was fortunate to receive a lottery grant of a million pounds for full restoration in recent years. The original design was for a lower tower and William Bidlake may have practiced his development of the bell tower when building St Patrick's in Salter Street. St Patrick's is not thought to have been built by the firm but there is a connection as the church is on adjoining land to Albert Bowen's farm at Lodge Paddocks in Earlswood and Albert may have employed William Bidlake to build an extension to Lodge Paddocks.

1901. Wesleyan Central Hall, Corporation Street, Birmingham.

Designed by Ewen Harper and listed as Grade 2*. This building replaced the first Central Hall and comprises shops on the ground floor and an internal worship area of gigantic proportions to meet the growing Wesleyan congregations. The seating capacity is for well over 2000. It is believed that at one time it was written into the articles of the Wesleyan Assurance Company that their A.G.M should be held at the Central Hall. The brick work was supplied by the Ketley Brick Company. The building is now used as a night club venue.

1902. Theatre Royal, New Street, Birmingham. (Mary Harding post card)

John Bowen & Sons extended the theatre building, a frontage of Portland stone.

1900. Pool at Woodcock Street Baths, Woodcock Street, Birmingham.

Designed by F.W. Lloyd with a Grade 2 listing. The cost of the extension which was opened in 1902 was £8,100. In 2010 Woodcock Street Baths was incorporated into Aston University and redeveloped following a major appeal.

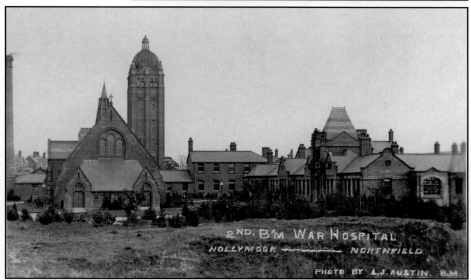

1900 -1905. Hollymoor Asylum, Rubery. (Mary Harding post card)

Designed by Martin and Chamberlain. The water tower and chapel are listed as Grade 2. Hollymoor was the first of two asylums built by the firm and each of which took five years to complete. The asylum initially provided for 600 patients and the contract was worth £207,256. The water tower, chapel and administration block is now all that remain.

The Hollymoor Asylum water tower with engine shed.
(Photo Matrix medical practice)

Eight skilled bricklayers were capable at that time of building five feet of the tower each day. The water tower, engine shed, chapel and administration block remain today and the tower can be seen from the M5 motorway when travelling between junctions 3 and 4

1905 - 1910 Netherne Asylum, Croydon, Surrey.
The laying of the foundation stone (Photo George Frogley)

Designed by George Hine. The hospital initially had accommodation for 960 patients and cost in the region of £300,000 to build. John Bowen can be seen facing us - the fifth from the left.

The former Netherne administration block as it is today (Photo George Frogley)

The administration block at Netherne. The hospital was vacated in 1995 and the administration block chapel and water tower are all that remain.

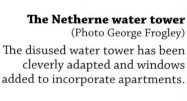

The Netherne water tower
(Photo George Frogley)

The disused water tower has been cleverly adapted and windows added to incorporate apartments.

One of five Foden's used by John Bowen & Sons.
(Photo The Road Locomotive Society)

There was not direct railway link to the site at Netherne and the firm bought five Foden Locomotives made in Sandbach for use in off loading building material from the railway spur.

1907. The Congregational Church, Ladypool Road Sparkbrook, Birmingham.

The lamp post on the right obscures foundation stones, one of which was laid by John Bowen's daughter, Florence Bowen. The church was built to incorporate a shop which is still in use today as a Charity shop.

1908 The Hurst, Amesbury Road, Moseley, Birmingham.

Designed by William Bidlake. The home of the author's grandfather Arthur Bowen, the second son of John Bowen and now owned by Birmingham City Council and divided into flats. An article on this superb house was included in the 13 December 1913 edition of Country Life.

1910. Hazelwell Wesleyan Methodist Church, Vicarage Road, Birmingham.
(Photo - Dennis and Margaret Hayes)

Designed by Ewen and Harper. This church was part of the extension of the Moseley Circuit and contributors to the building costs included the General Manager of the Wesleyan Assurance Society, R. A. Hunt, who contributed £250, John Bowen £150, and Arthur Bowen £15. The church has now been demolished.

1910. Nechells Baths,at the corner of Nechells Park Road and Aston Church Road.

Designed by Arthur Harrison and listed as Grade 2. The building fell into disrepair and closed in 1995. Following a £5.5 million refurbishment it was restored to its former glory in 2012.

1910. Hockley Post Office, Hockley Hill, Birmingham.

Designed by Edward Cropper. During the planning and construction of the building, it was decided to fit a pneumatic tube between this office and the Head Post Office in Victoria Square to convey telegrams for the Messenger Boys to deliver. This cut out the need for an instrument room at Hockley so that room was used for other purposes.

The Post Office is now closed but the sorting office at the rear, which was also built by the firm, is still in use.

1913 - The Birmingham Repertory Theatre, Station Street, Birmingham.

Designed by S.N. Cooke and Partners. Sir Barry Jackson's theatre was built in just four months between October 1912 and February 1913. The design was based on the Kunstler Theatre in Munich and was the first purpose built Repertory Theatre in this Country.

1914. The extension to The Queen's Hotel, Stephenson Street.
(Photo - Mary Harding post card)

The extension can be seen on the right hand side. The hotel is now demolished.

1917. The Lychgate to St Anne's Church, Park Hill Moseley.

Built in memory of John Bowen's year as High Sheriff. A marble plaque in the church includes his son Leslie Bowen's name with some thirty two other Moseley men who died in the Great War.

1922. The Baptistery of St Anne's Park Hill Moseley.

The baptistery was donated by John Bowen in thanksgiving for his long happy and successful life. The baptistery suffered severe damage when the church was bombed on the 3 December 1940 and was subsequently restored.

1923. The Colonnade and site of The Hall of Memory, Centenary Square, Birmingham. (Mary Harding post card).

Three builders were involved with this site for the Hall of Memory designed by S. N. Cooke and J. W. Twist and is listed as Grade 2. John Barnsley & Sons built the Hall of Memory, John Bowen & Sons laid out the grounds and built the Memorial Colonnade and Messrs Fennings of London built the marble shrine and seats. The Colonnade was moved and re-erected in the Peace Gardens next to St Thomas's Church in Bath Row in 1989.

It was appropriate that the building work was shared as both John Bowen and John Barnsley each lost a son in the Great War.

1930's. Moseley Telephone Exchange, Moseley Road, Birmingham.

It is possible that John Bowen & Sons built both the Post Office and the sorting office at the rear.

1930's houses in Russell Road, Moseley, Birmingham.

Members of the family lived in Russell Road and the firm almost certainly built houses in this road.

1937. The Beacon Insurance Building Stratford Road, Hall Green, Birmingham.

Designed by T. Wynne Thomas of Nicol, Nicol and Thomas architects.

This building has a distinctive Art Deco feel, and is now used as serviced offices.

1939. St Edward's Roman Catholic Church, Raddlebarn Road, Selly Park, Birmingham.

John Bowen & Sons built the extension to this church.

1939 -1945 World War Two Prefabs.

During the Second World War, the firm had extensive contracts with the Government and erected prefabs in Birmingham and assembled Romney huts at army camps and on airfields at Honeybourne and Long Marston in Warwickshire, and at Bicester and Nesscliff.

1959. The Midland Bank, Station Road, Dorridge, Warwickshire.

The firm had extensive contracts with the Midland Bank, but this building is a sad reflection of the heady days of The Victoria Law Courts.

1963. Five Ways Erdington, Birmingham.

John Bowen & Sons Ltd, had a sub contract from Rex Ford builders of Shirley for a shopping precinct in Erdington and it was the last job the firm had before it went into administration in 1963. Brian Larkins of Price Waterhouse was the administrator.